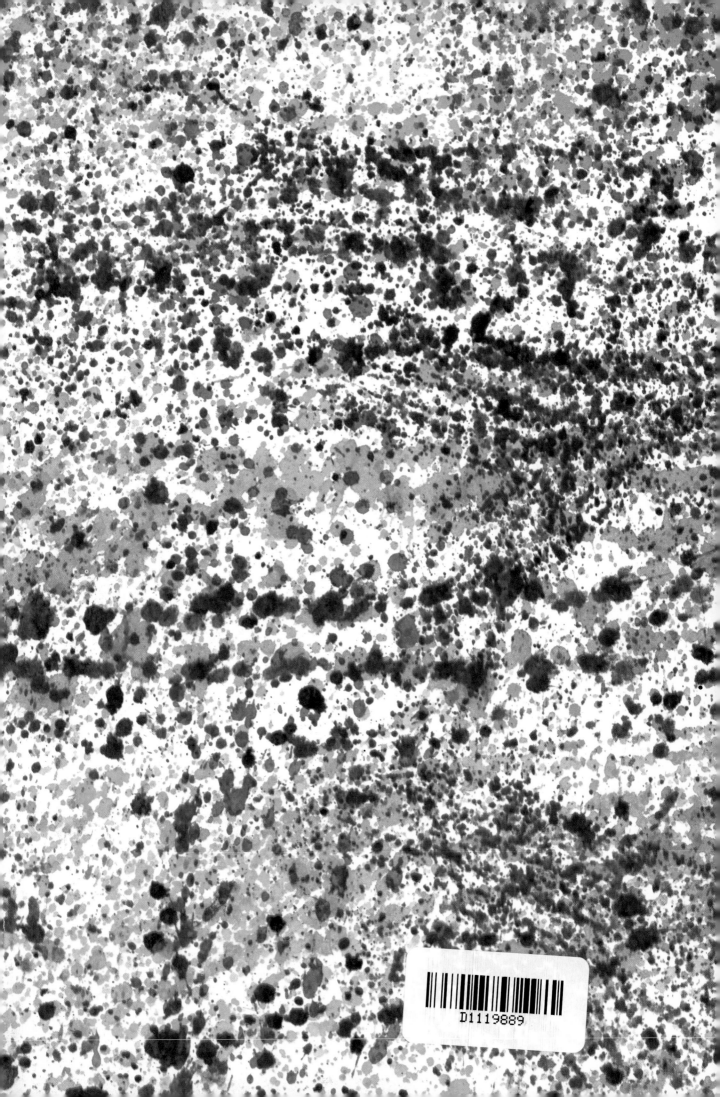

Library of Congress Cataloging in Publication Data
Fisher, Aileen Lucia, date   Do bears have mothers, too?   SUMMARY: A collection of short
poems about baby animals includes "Penguin Chick," "Baby Monkey," and "Alligator Children."
[1. Animals—Poetry]   I. Carle, Eric.   II. Title   PZ8.3.F634Mz
811'.5'2   73-4721   ISBN 0-690-00166-5   ISBN 0-690-00167-3 (lib. bdg.)

10   9   8   7   6   5   4   3   2

Do Bears Have Mothers, Too?
Aileen Fisher/Eric Carle

Thomas Y. Crowell Company · New York

Little Deer

Here, little fawn,
in the dappled green
is a place you can lie
and not be seen.

You can't tag along
with legs so thin,
and I haven't a pocket
to put you in.

So gather strength
as you hide, my fawn,
and I'll come feed you
at dusk and dawn.

And pretty soon
in the mild June weather
off we'll romp
through the woods together.

The Swans

Cygnets, you must practice early
not to be unkempt or surly.
Swans have quite a reputation—
we are known in every nation
for our grace and stately beauty.
To uphold this is your duty.

So, if swimming makes you weary,
you can still look chic and cheery:
climb upon my back—I ask it,
with my wings I'll make a basket
where you're bound to look sedate
as we move along in state.

Elephant Child

Elephant child,
you're called a calf
like the child of a dolphin
or giraffe.

But, elephant calf,
you're much more grand—
you've a flexible trunk
like a flexible hand

For plucking food
from the top of a tree,
or taking a shower
conveniently.

You'll do great things
with that wonderful nose,
but I'll tweak your ears
if you tickle my toes!

Joey Kangaroo

You're a lucky young one, Joey:
if it's cloudy out, or blowy,
you just cuddle in my pouch
on a velvet-covered couch.

When I'm bounding off, or leaping,
you ride with me in safe-keeping,
closed inside or peeking out
as we make our way about.

And no matter where we roam,
dinner's always there — at home.
Yes, you're lucky, son. Be merry!
Soon you'll be too big to carry.

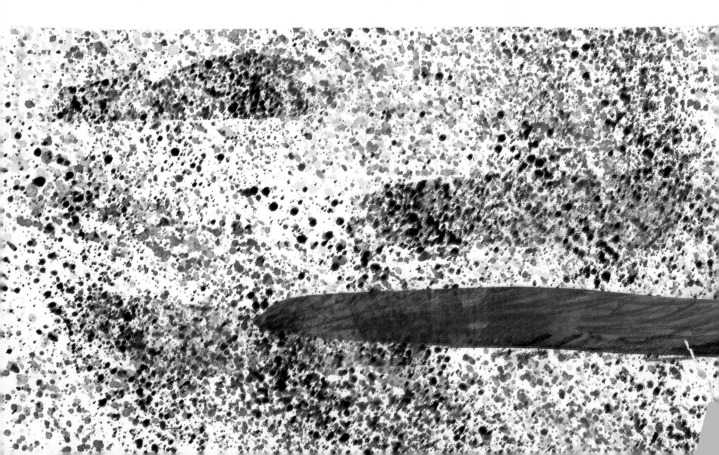

Bear Cubs

Come, little cub,
don't look so sad.
One little spank
is all you had.
You *know* that teasing
your twin is bad.

Come, little cub,
don't look so blue.
One little spank
is nothing new.
I love you both—
you *know* I do.

And I know where
there's a special tree
with honey enough
for one, two, three,
so, come, little cubs,
and follow me.

Penguin Chick

Your father and I, my penguin chick,
think bringing-up-children far from quick.

Your father stood with your egg tucked in
his pocket-y fold of soft warm skin
for *sixty days* — and he got quite thin.

Then just as you were starting to hatch,
I brought you squid, a digested batch.

For several weeks in the cold and storm,
you ate "fish soup" while I kept you warm.

So now it's great that at last you're able
to stand so sturdy and straight and stable
and eat real fish at the "dinner table."

Alligator Children

Listen, my children, my very own,
you're still too young to go off alone.

You might get lost, or you might get caught
and sold to tourists—a dreadful thought.

I watched and waited for two months straight
for the eggs you were in to incubate.

And then the minute you cried, distressed,
I dug you out of the leaf-mound nest.

So ride on my back and stay a while,
and I'll go around with a toothy smile.

Baby Giraffe

When you get big, my beautiful calf,
you'll be more tall than tall-and-a-half.
No one's as tall as a grown giraffe.

And nobody blends so perfectly
with a sunlit grove...so it's hard to see
what spots are giraffe and what are tree.

But now you're small, and you hardly know,
my pet, where your legs and your neck should go.
I'll give you a nudge and help you—so!

Up on your stilts, your neck in the sky!
You *have* to stand tall with your head held high;
your dinner is waiting up here, that's why.

Baby Monkey

Hold on tight,
my little one.
Up we'll climb,
and off we'll run.

Grip your fingers,
press your knees,
and we'll gambol
through the trees.

If you can't
cling tight enough,
I'll hold you
when the going's rough.

And all night long
we'll clasp each other,
one small baby
and its mother.

Little Foxes

You mustn't go out, my pups, to play—
at least for a while, perhaps all day.

Someone's around with a dog and gun…
you mustn't go out to romp and run!

Stay quietly here inside the den
till the woods and meadow are safe again,

Till the scent is gone and the air is still
and the jays are silent below the hill.

Dolphin Daughter

Dolphin daughter,
in the water
we will swim and play,
swerve together,
curve together
all the green-lit day.

We'll tease turtles
with our hurtles
as we hurry past;
we'll scare fishes
with our swishes...
don't grow up too fast!

Lion Cubs

Possums have a pocket
and kangaroos a pouch
where they can carry babies
as they walk or run or crouch.

I haven't pouch or pocket
to tote you north or south,
and so, my cubs, I carry you
a-dangling from my mouth.

I let you maul and tease me
and pounce upon my tail
and badger me when I'm asleep
and "scare" me on the trail.

I try to teach you manners,
I fondle you, and play,
and hope when *you* have cubs to raise
you'll do it just that way.